Wise Words from Victor Hugo

RICHARD CAMERON

Copyright © 2014 Richard Cameron

All rights reserved.

ISBN: 1502555476
ISBN-13: 978-1502555472

DISCLAIMER

While every effort has been made to ensure the information in this book is correct, human error is always a possibility and therefore the author cannot accept responsibility for any inaccuracies.

CONTENTS

Introduction	1
About Himself	3
Education	5
General Philosophy	7
God, Prayer & Religion	13
Happiness, Love & Beauty	19
Humankind	25
War, Revolution, Justice & Freedom	29
Life, Aging & Death	35
Literature & Music	39
Suffering	41
Wise Sayings	43
Women	49

INTRODUCTION

Victor Hugo (1802 – 1885) was one of the nineteenth century's great thinkers. Remembered today in the English speaking world particularly for his novels *Les Misérables* and *The Hunchback of Notre Dame*, he was in his own time a campaigner for social justice, an admirer of Napoleon and supporter of the revolutions that rocked France and ushered in a new era. He was also a poet, for which he is still highly revered in France, a skilled artist, playwright, philosopher and politician.

He campaigned tirelessly for human rights and his calls for the abolition of the death penalty, not just in France but around the world, mark him out as a forward thinker, ahead of his time. Although a believer in God, he rejected organised religion and called himself a freethinker. The influence of his writings on the French public was, and remains, profound; and outside of France also his messages about justice, the legal system, poverty and women's rights as well as on a host of other issues continue to have relevance to our world.

That Victor Hugo was a man for all times and all people is demonstrated vividly in the quotations from his writings contained in this book. Read them, reflect on them and ask questions arising from them.

ABOUT HIMSELF

"I love all men who think, even those who think otherwise than myself."

*

"My tastes are aristocratic, my actions democratic."

*

"I am a soul. I know well that what I shall render up to the grave is not myself. That which is myself will go elsewhere. Earth, thou art not my abyss!"

*

RICHARD CAMERON

"Men like me are impossible until the day when they become necessary."

*

"I am an intelligent river which has reflected successively all the banks before which it has flowed by meditating only on the images offered by those changing shores."

*

"I'm religiously opposed to religion."

EDUCATION

"He who opens a school door, closes a prison."

*

"The learned man knows that he is ignorant."

*

"The man who does not know other languages, unless he is a man of genius, necessarily has deficiencies in his ideas."

*

"An intelligent hell would be better than a stupid paradise."

*

"Common sense is in spite of, not as the result of education."

*

"Intelligence is the wife, imagination is the mistress, memory is the servant."

*

"To learn to read is to light a fire; every syllable that is spelled out is a spark."

GENERAL PHILOSOPHY

"What would be ugly in a garden constitutes beauty in a mountain."

*

"Strange to say, the luminous world is the invisible world; the luminous world is that which we do not see. Our eyes of flesh see only night."

*

"There is one spectacle grander than the sea, that is the sky; there is one spectacle grander than the sky, that is the interior of the soul."

*

"Fashions have done more harm than revolutions."

*

"All the forces in the world are not so powerful as an idea whose time has come."

*

"Thought is the labour of the intellect, reverie is its pleasure."

*

"Doing nothing is happiness for children and misery for old men."

*

"Everything being a constant carnival, there is no carnival left."

*

"Style is the substance of the subject called unceasingly to the surface."

*

"Nations, like stars, are entitled to eclipse. All is well, provided the light returns and the eclipse does not become endless night. Dawn and resurrection are synonymous. The reappearance of the light is the same as the survival of the soul."

*

"Each man should frame life so that at some future hour fact and his dreaming meet."

*

"No one ever keeps a secret so well as a child."

*

"One is not idle because one is absorbed. There is both visible and invisible labour. To contemplate is to toil, to think is to do. The crossed arms work, the clasped hands act. The eyes upturned to Heaven are an act of creation."

*

"What is history? An echo of the past in the future; a reflex from the future on the past."

*

"Change your opinions, keep to your principles; change your leaves, keep intact your roots."

*

"To contemplate is to look at shadows."

*

"Men become accustomed to poison by degrees."

*

"There is a sacred horror about everything grand. It is easy to admire mediocrity and hills; but whatever is too lofty, a genius as well as a mountain, an assembly as well as a masterpiece, seen too near, is appalling."

*

"Be as a bird perched on a frail branch that she feels bending beneath her, still she sings away all the same, knowing she has wings."

*

"Have courage for the great sorrows of life and patience for the small ones; and when you have laboriously accomplished your daily task, go to sleep in peace."

*

"The animal is ignorant of the fact that he knows. The man is aware of the fact that he is ignorant."

*

"Architecture has recorded the great ideas of the human race. Not only every religious symbol, but every human thought has its page in that vast book."

*

"Genius: the superhuman in man."

*

"Be like the bird who, pausing in her flight awhile on boughs too slight, feels them give way beneath her, and yet sings, knowing she hath wings."

*

"Genius is a promontory jutting out into the infinite."

GOD, PRAYER & RELIGION

"The human soul has still greater need of the ideal than of the real. It is by the real that we exist; it is by the ideal that we live."

*

"Jesus wept; Voltaire smiled. From that divine tear and from that human smile is derived the grace of present civilization."

*

"When God desires to destroy a thing, he entrusts its destruction to the thing itself. Every bad institution of this world ends by suicide."

*

"To give thanks in solitude is enough. Thanksgiving has wings and goes where it must go. Your prayer knows much more about it than you do."

*

"The word is the Verb, and the Verb is God."

*

"A faith is a necessity to a man. Woe to him who believes in nothing."

*

"The soul has illusions as the bird has wings: it is supported by them."

*

"There are thoughts which are prayers. There are

moments when, whatever the posture of the body, the soul is on its knees."

*

"Prayer is an august avowal of ignorance."

*

"Indigestion is charged by God with enforcing morality on the stomach."

*

"Toleration is the best religion."

*

"To think is of itself to be useful; it is always and in all cases a striving toward God."

*

"Because one doesn't like the way things are is no

reason to be unjust towards God."

*

"Blessed be Providence which has given to each his toy: the doll to the child, the child to the woman, the woman to the man, the man to the devil!"

*

"Hope is the word which God has written on the brow of every man."

*

"Conscience is God present in man."

*

"Hell is an outrage on humanity. When you tell me that your deity made you in his image, I reply that he must have been very ugly."

*

"Religions do a useful thing: they narrow God to the limits of man. Philosophy replies by doing a necessary thing: it elevates man to the plane of God."

HAPPINESS, LOVE & BEAUTY

"There are fathers who do not love their children; there is no grandfather who does not adore his grandson."

*

"Joy's smile is much closer to tears than laughter."

*

"To love is to act."

*

"Love is a portion of the soul itself, and it is of the same nature as the celestial breathing of the atmosphere of paradise."

*

"Sublime upon sublime scarcely presents a contrast, and we need a little rest from everything, even the beautiful."

*

"The most powerful symptom of love is a tenderness which becomes at times almost insupportable."

*

"To be perfectly happy it does not suffice to possess happiness, it is necessary to have deserved it."

*

"What a grand thing, to be loved! What a grander thing still, to love!"

*

"I met in the street a very poor young man who was in love. His hat was old, his coat worn, his cloak was out at the elbows, the water passed through his shoes, - and the stars through his soul."

*

"To love beauty is to see light."

*

"Laughter is the sun that drives winter from the human face."

*

"The greatest happiness of life is the conviction that we are loved; loved for ourselves, or rather, loved in spite of ourselves."

*

"Dear God! how beauty varies in nature and art. In a woman the flesh must be like marble; in a statue the marble must be like flesh."

*

"Life is the flower for which love is the honey."

*

"The first symptom of love in a young man is timidity; in a girl boldness."

*

"To love another person is to see the face of God."

*

"Son, brother, father, lover, friend. There is room in the heart for all the affections, as there is room in heaven for all the stars."

*

"How did it happen that their lips came together? How does it happen that birds sing, that snow melts, that the rose unfolds, that the dawn whitens behind the stark shapes of trees on the quivering summit of the hill? A kiss, and all was said."

*

"Try as you will, you cannot annihilate that eternal relic of the human heart, love."

*

"The beautiful has but one type, the ugly has a thousand."

*

"The ideal and the beautiful are identical; the ideal corresponds to the idea, and beauty to form; hence idea and substance are cognate."

HUMANKIND

"The little people must be sacred to the big ones, and it is from the rights of the weak that the duty of the strong is comprised."

*

"Our acts make or mar us, we are the children of our own deeds."

*

"Smallness in a great man seems smaller by its disproportion with all the rest."

*

"Adversity makes men, and prosperity makes monsters."

*

"Well, for us, in history where goodness is a rare pearl, he who was good almost takes precedence over he who was great."

*

"It is most pleasant to commit a just action which is disagreeable to someone whom one does not like."

*

"The mountains, the forest, and the sea, render men savage; they develop the fierce, but yet do not destroy the human."

*

"People do not lack strength; they lack will."

"The wicked envy and hate; it is their way of admiring."

*

"One of the hardest tasks is to extract continually from one's soul an almost inexhaustible ill will."

*

"Mankind is not a circle with a single center but an ellipse with two focal points of which facts are one and ideas the other."

*

"Almost all our desires, when examined, contain something too shameful to reveal."

*

"Society is a republic. When an individual tries to lift themselves above others, they are dragged down by the mass, either by ridicule or slander."

*

"One believes others will do what he will do to himself."

*

"Great perils have this beauty, that they bring to light the fraternity of strangers."

WAR, REVOLUTION, JUSTICE & FREEDOM

"Liberation is not deliverance."

*

"I don't mind what Congress does, as long as they don't do it in the streets and frighten the horses."

*

"When liberty returns, I will return."

*

"There have been in this century only one great man and one great thing: Napoleon and liberty. For want of the great man, let us have the great thing."

*

"A creditor is worse than a slave-owner; for the master owns only your person, but a creditor owns your dignity, and can command it."

*

"Civil war? What does that mean? Is there any foreign war? Isn't every war fought between men, between brothers?"

*

"We say that slavery has vanished from European civilization, but this is not true. Slavery still exists, but now it applies only to women and its name is prostitution."

*

"Freedom in art, freedom in society, this is the double goal towards which all consistent and logical minds must strive."

*

"He who is not capable of enduring poverty is not capable of being free."

*

"Peace is the virtue of civilization. War is its crime."

*

"As a means of contrast with the sublime, the grotesque is, in our view, the richest source that nature can offer."

*

"The last resort of kings, the cannonball. The last resort of the people, the paving stone."

*

"It is the end. But of what? The end of France? No. The end of kings? Yes."

*

"The brutalities of progress are called revolutions. When they are over we realize this: that the human race has been roughly handled, but that it has advanced."

*

"Amnesty is as good for those who give it as for those who receive it. It has the admirable quality of bestowing mercy on both sides."

*

"The omnipotence of evil has never resulted in anything but fruitless efforts. Our thoughts always escape from whoever tries to smother them."

*

"Despotism is a long crime."

*

"A war between Europeans is a civil war."

*

"When dictatorship is a fact, revolution becomes a right."

*

"Close by the Rights of Man, at the least set beside them, are the Rights of the Spirit."

*

"Evil. Mistrust those who rejoice at it even more than those who do it."

*

"Those who live are those who fight."

LIFE, AGING & DEATH

"Our life dreams the Utopia. Our death achieves the Ideal."

"Short as life is, we make it still shorter by the careless waste of time."

*

"Forty is the old age of youth; fifty the youth of old age."

*

"Whenever a man's friends begin to compliment him about looking young, he may be sure that they think he is growing old."

*

"It is nothing to die. It is frightful not to live."

*

"One sometimes says: 'He killed himself because he was bored with life.' One ought rather to say: 'He killed himself because he was bored by lack of life.'"

*

"The wise man does not grow old, but ripens."

*

"When grace is joined with wrinkles, it is adorable. There is an unspeakable dawn in happy old age."

*

"We see past time in a telescope and present time in a microscope. Hence the apparent enormities of the present."

LITERATURE & MUSIC

"The ode lives upon the ideal, the epic upon the grandiose, the drama upon the real."

*

"The drama is complete poetry. The ode and the epic contain it only in germ; it contains both of them in a state of high development, and epitomizes both."

*

"Music expresses that which cannot be said and on which it is impossible to be silent."

*

"A library implies an act of faith."

*

"I put a Phrygian cap on the old dictionary."

*

"Rhyme, that enslaved queen, that supreme charm of our poetry, that creator of our meter."

*

"It is from books that wise people derive consolation in the troubles of life."

SUFFERING

"It is by suffering that human beings become angels."

*

"Pain is as diverse as man. One suffers as one can."

*

"The three great problems of this century; the degradation of man in the proletariat, the subjection of women through hunger, the atrophy of the child by darkness."

*

"The ox suffers, the cart complains."

*

"Sorrow is a fruit. God does not make it grow on limbs too weak to bear it."

WISE SAYINGS

"A compliment is something like a kiss through a veil."

*

"Stupidity talks, vanity acts."

*

"There is nothing like a dream to create the future."

*

"Do not let it be your aim to be something, but to be someone."

*

"Strong and bitter words indicate a weak cause."

*

"The flesh is the surface of the unknown."

*

"Idleness is the heaviest of all oppressions."

*

"Habit is the nursery of errors."

*

"Taste is the common sense of genius."

*

"A great artist is a great man in a great child."

*

"To rise from error to truth is rare and beautiful."

*

"Reaction - a boat which is going against the current but which does not prevent the river from flowing on."

*

"To think of shadows is a serious thing."

*

"He, who every morning plans the transactions of the day, and follows that plan, carries a thread that will guide him through a labyrinth of the most busy life."

*

"Never laugh at those who suffer; suffer sometimes those who laugh."

*

"There is no such thing as a little country. The greatness of a people is no more determined by their numbers than the greatness of a man is by his height."

*

"Concision in style, precision in thought, decision in life."

*

"When a man is out of sight, it is not too long before he is out of mind."

*

"Perseverance, secret of all triumphs."

*

"As the purse is emptied, the heart is filled."

*

"By putting forward the hands of the clock you shall not advance the hour."

*

"Initiative is doing the right thing without being told."

*

"Wisdom is a sacred communion."

*

"One sees qualities at a distance and defects at close range."

*

"Virtue has a veil, vice a mask."

*

"Puns are the droppings of soaring wits."

*

"Many great actions are committed in small struggles."

*

"Scepticism, that dry caries of the intelligence."

WOMEN

"A mother's arms are made of tenderness and children sleep soundly in them."

*

"When a woman is talking to you, listen to what she says with her eyes."

*

"Without vanity, without coquetry, without curiosity, in a word, without the fall, woman would not be woman. Much of her grace is in her frailty."

*

"Curiosity is one of the forms of feminine bravery."

*

"Nature has made a pebble and a female. The lapidary makes the diamond, and the lover makes the woman."

*

"No one knows like a woman how to say things which are at once gentle and deep."

*

"It is often necessary to know how to obey a woman in order sometimes to have the right to command her."

WISE WORDS FROM VICTOR HUGO

# RICHARD CAMERON

ALSO BY RICHARD CAMERON

THOUGHTS OF THOREAU

UKIP'S PARTY POOPERS

Made in the USA
Middletown, DE
14 January 2019